I0811024

First Light, Last Light

Praise for First Light, Last Light

"Glen Sorestad first came to prominence back in the '70s, writing prairie pub poems. In 2000, he (became) Canada's first provincial poet laureate, and since then, he has continued crafting fine poems full of telling details and warm humanity. In First Light, Last Light, *he writes with sensitivity about friends and family, the present and the past. He knows the human situation where people often carom through relationships like discs in games of crokinole. He understands the power of nature as crows and catbirds, jays and juncos, waxwings and chickadees flutter through his poems . . . Yes, Glen Sorestad is still writing poems that will delight readers."*

— Robert Currie, Saskatchewan's second poet laureate

"Glen Sorestad's poems range widely in time and space yet ground themselves in an attentive dedication to the local, to home's dailiness: a red fox on the back lawn, 'vocal tabernacle' of robins, a snowy owl that causes a traffic jam in an urban mall's entrance. Alongside loss and grief lives wonder, joy. The snowy owl poem's final lines aptly encapsulate Sorestad's poetic vision: "hope manifests itself/in unexpected places, in wee but wondrous ways."

— Jeanette Lynes, Author of *Bedlam Cowslip: The John Clare Poems*

First Light, Last Light

SHADOWPAW PRESS

New poetry by

Glen Sorestad

FIRST LIGHT, LAST LIGHT
By Glen Sorestad

Shadowpaw Press
Regina, Saskatchewan, Canada
www.shadowpawpress.com

Trade Paperback ISBN: 978-1-998273-46-1
Ebook ISBN: 978-1-998273-47-8

Shadowpaw Press is grateful for
the financial support of Creative Saskatchewan.

CREATIVE SASKATCHEWAN

Table of Contents

Part 1: The Human Touch

Part 2: Sunbeams and Shadows

Dedicated to my children,
grandchildren and
great-grandchildren

Part One

The Human Touch

Once

Once
there were
two boys who
thought the sun rose
and set on their dad;
sometimes they were certain
their dad controlled its rising
and its setting. Later they saw
he had become first light and last light;
when he died, they were left only darkness.

A Straightener of Nails

Whenever my father spotted a nail no longer true
and discarded as useless, he always picked up
the reject to carry along with him

to where he kept an old tobacco can,
where the off-kilter joined the collection of cripples
needing his attention. It was a task for another day.

I was too young to understand his reason for doing this,
nor to fathom what satisfaction he received for his
slow and deliberate care in returning each nail to true.

This was when my father's livelihood was driving
his car down gravel or dirt roads selling Fuller brushes,
then Electrolux vacuums, Nutty Club confectioneries.

He eked a meagre wage, but his heart was never in it.
His honesty and regard for others road-blocked sales
and he could never pressure anyone to buy.

Rainy weekends, I would find him in his workshop,
happy with his hammer and his tobacco can, working
against time to set things true, the only way he could.

January 17th

I don't know why I remembered Mother's birthday,
especially when my memory has sprung more holes
than a bullet-riddled prairie stop sign; and considering
that she has been gone over twenty-five years now
and were she alive to celebrate this birthday,
she would be one hundred seventeen years young.
But mothers never grow old.

They never die either. Mothers are always with us,
always present, in the words that leap unbidden from
our mouths; in the manner we wield a potato peeler,
or tie our shoelaces; in a host of melodies that hum
and have been imbedded into the fibre of who we are.

Some days, I am almost certain I hear her voice,
arguing with herself, as I recall from childhood.
But of course, I realize the voice is my own,
just as I recognize why I have and will remember,
as far as my memory will take me,
the importance of this mid-winter day.

A Wooden Spoon

. . . for Delmar

My boyhood friend recently gifted me an ordinary wooden kitchen spoon, worn with years of turning and mixing and folding; the kind of spoon that conjures up memories of mothers and baking, warm kitchens, delectable wafts of cinnamon or cloves, the fidgety wait to lick the last remnants of chocolate or sugar cookie batter from the hand-carved wood. Each old wooden spoon stirs and ladles its own epics and anecdotes, its own whispered endearments or sharp-tongued reproofs, the sad, salt taste of tears.

An unusual gift, perhaps—two men in the autumn of their lives, friends more than sixty years. The timing makes the act rarer still. Widowed less than a year, he gave me the spoon at a memorial gathering for his wife. Out of loss, recovery. Out of recovery, memory.

My friend had unearthed the spoon while clearing rubble and remnants of the nearby family farm which holds my childhood and adolescence. Out of destruction, resurrection. On the upper side of the palm smoothed handle a bold hand etched or carved, *Myrtle.* On the handle's back side—*January 17, 1932.* A small heart is carved through the handle's end, an opening to hang the spoon, a hook to hang a heart on.

The heart is more than a convenience. This gift, more than an act of kindness. I turn the spoon in my hands, run my fingers over this twice-given gift, older than I am, as if to rub this wood with vigour might invoke my mother back to brighten my life. Memories hold me firm, my hands hold this spoon. The carved date, my mother's twenty-sixth birthday.

Kicking the Habit

My mother smoked cigarettes
until she reached her seventies,
until one day she chanced to glance
in the mirror and the image startled her,
cigarette clenched between her lips,
the thin grey waft of poison
curling upwards. What she saw
was an old woman, smoking,
and she recognized it wasn't pretty.

A shutter clicked, a bulb flashed
and she hated the mirror snapshot.
That day she quit, cold turkey,
never smoked again in her life.
She lived into her ninety-third year,
so how much the tobacco
shortened her life is moot.

I asked her how hard it had been
to cure an addiction grown
over a half-century and she said
whenever the urge to smoke
seized her, all the resolve
she needed lay in that image:
old woman with a fag hanging
from the corner of her mouth.

1935 Ford

I close my eyes and I can
still see him behind the wheel
of a green '35 Ford,
his grey Fedora tilted just so,
a suggestion of debonair,
both hands thumbs up
on the steering wheel,
a lifetime habit learned
from herding gravel trucks
with primitive steering
on the washboard roads
trekking those treeless plains.

But most of all, I can see
his smile, the easy grin of a man
at home behind the wheel,
his view of the world panoramic,
a great rolling vista,
humming to himself and smiling,
scrutinizing the standstill world
as if it were his feudal manor,
the driver's seat his throne.

Always Your Child

No matter how long ago
that whimpering baby you first held,
afraid you might somehow drop
on the hospital maternity ward floor;

that chunky diapered scamp,
not yet two, who followed his mom
all day, calling her "Honey",
amazed to discover the radio
would always play the same songs
his mom was singing, wanting to know
how the radio knew which song
she was going to sing;

the four-year old in the family car
enunciating in phonetic perfection:
Uni-vers-itas Sas-kat-chew-an-sis
as we entered the campus gate,
stunning our next-door neighbour
along for the ride;

the almost nine-year-old who boarded
a city bus to ride alone
to a distant school for the gifted;
the same boy four years later
sitting with a same-age classmate
beneath a dessert table festooned
with goodies at a welcoming event
for freshies to high school;

the same child, four years later
and now over six feet tall,
bound for a law degree,
a life partner he'd already chosen,
passing up on a year of travel
in Europe, his eye fixed
on getting on with life,
whatever he deemed that to be,
ready to take on whatever
life was about to hand him.

Life blessed him with three boys,
and we, as grandparents, doted
as we ought to have, gladly
melding into our second go-round
experiencing the wondrous metamorphosis
of babies becoming six-footers.

Their father was still our child,
just as he was to become
father of his towering trio.
But though father, still child.

Though he should have stood
alongside our graves, when our time
had come, our first child upset
the natural order and preceded us
to that final mystery.

But a child is ever a child
and to lose one, lose one at any
stage in life, is grievous, a wound
that never leaves—having no place to go.

Blues Concert

The bluesman uncases his guitar
from its well-travelled case
and slides it slowly onto his lap,

avoiding obstructions on this tiny stage
available to him for this very special
one-time performance.

His nimble fingers run routine warm-up
chords and string soundings; he makes
minor tuning tweaks until

at last, his ear is satisfied. His listener,
all this while, is silent, motionless,
but eyes alive, anticipating.

The bluesman opens with a song tailored
to his audience, the man with whom he has
spent time and whom he has

come to know as a good friend. One by one,
he moves through his planned set of songs
and each becomes an act of love

he knows his friend will recognize. He also
knows this solo gig is the last time he will
ever see his friend.

Within cramped confines of this cancer ward room,
the bluesman wails against life's injustices.
Wetness glistens in the eyes of the friend

he almost failed to recognize, the cancer
had so altered him since they last met.
The final notes fade away.

The patient has done his best to applaud
despite the web of tubes and wires
that sustain him in his final days.

The bluesman embraces the patient,
whispering "Godspeed, my friend"
before he leaves the hospital room.

The patient sinks back onto his pillows,
closes his eyes, the drugs flow. The only sounds
are the machinery of medicine.

The Things We Have to Learn

You are a family man, a lifer, have
partnered in the raising of four children,
adults now with their own children.

You believe you know these children
you are quite proud to call your own.
But nothing is ever so certain as it appears.

Death lays a grim hand on the shoulder
of one of your own and you are shaken
to realize how paltry your knowledge.

The nearer the final breath of your child
the more you learn you did not know.
You believe, too, if this is true of one,

it must also be true of all the others.
You are parents who knew naught.
But you also believe this: despite all

of which you are ignorant, you know
as do they, how much you have loved
each with unhidden and unbidden joy.

What I Want to Tell My Late Son's Three Sons

I know your Dad is gone from your life a full year
and you wonder just what you are expected to feel,

now that you have passed this unwanted moment
in your early lives. I've been where you are and I

may not know much about how we best honor
the father whom Death has stolen. But I do know this:

it is quite all right if you are unable to think about
your Dad, whenever you are alone, without tears.

Even if you have not yet cried through your loss,
just know that the time for those tears is unlimited,

that they may be prompted forth when you
least expect them. That, too, is quite all right.

There will be times when this absence will appear
as a fierce ache that will not leave, as if you've lost

an arm or leg. Just know, this is all part of who
you are, of who you will always be. One day, you

will share stories with your own sons or daughters
about the grandfather they will never get to know.

You will be telling them, without using the words,
how much you miss him, how much you loved him.

Missing a father is normal. It has no expiry date.

Honouring Our Fathers

My wife and I, comparing notes about
our long-departed fathers, were surprised
to realize that despite both having

emerged from quite different European
immigrant cultures, the two men were
nonetheless remarkably similar, sharing

little idiosyncratic habits, each had adopted
as environmental offshoots of lean
and hungry pioneer boyhoods.

Born into large homesteader families
in Canada, or in my father's case,
in the United States—my father,

a decade older than my wife's—
they both acquired and realized
the intrinsic need and value of family.

Both preached with verve the honest
dignity of work. As young men, they
had survived the First World War,

the Spanish Flu, the Great Depression,
then War Two. Both our fathers were
consistent in the ingrained habit

of ensuring, at the meal's close,
their plates hardly warranted washing,
so thoroughly had they wielded

their remaining bread crusts to sop up
every edible ort. Now that our own
children have empty-nested us,

we no longer cook large meals and are
well removed from starvation,
or having to stretch the food budget,

as necessity had demanded of us earlier.
At meal's end we realize we have
now become our fathers: each of whom

takes over, as we break off a final
chunk or slice of bread and leave
our plates cleaned of the merest morsel.

One June Day in Normandy

. . . remembering Ernest Dalshaug

It is June 6th again. A stirring inside,
I am missing something that matters—
the uncle I never knew. It hurts.

Though I age and time past grows fainter,
I have always been aware of this:
the missing are always missed.

Juno Beach, 1944. History is a message
written in blood for those who survive.
Ernie died that day. D-Day.

Canadian troops stormed the breakers
from landing crafts into the readied defenses --
Juno Beach ran scarlet with blood.

Who knows whether he even reached shore—
so many didn't—drowned, or downed by fire.
The history of war: always incomplete.

Did Death come quick? The record is mute.
Numbers are the fodder of History.
Facts are devoid of emotion.

Just twenty-two, he fell. A Normandy grave
holds what remains of his great adventure,
over before it could truly begin.

The Canadian War Cemetery: *Beny Sur Mer*
holds what was left at day's end.
A grave, so many empty hearts.

Road Trip

1.

I've always felt there was no place I'd rather be
than behind the steering wheel of a sound car,
an ever-changing landscape flashing past.

I have been doing just this, off and on, now
for close to seventy years and while age has
braked desire a tad, the next trip still revs me.

My back complains, as do my legs. They insist
they will not tolerate road marathons of the past.
I heed them, though I consider them wimps.

My father spent much of his working life, hands
firm to a wheel—gravel trucks, roiling dust clouds;
or lumber trucks, pitching down precipitous slopes.

He ended up on rural roads, watching the world
pass by, peddling home brushes or vacuums,
eyeballing crops, always ahead of a dust plume.

2.

Though I admired all he'd been for me
and though I had no inkling of my destiny,
I never had a desire to become my father.

I knew a salesman's life was not for me.
Selling held zero appeal for a teen who saw
on the horizon a career as a pro ballplayer.

But it's clear my father passed via his genes,
or in the stories he told, his fierce love of
being behind the wheel, rolling through

an ever-changing geography and geology
and history, rapt and captivated as viewer.
I understood why he loved it as he did.

3.

I still have the growing anticipation that singes
the edges of my patience each time my wife
and I set off on another road trip, I am at ease

only after I slide behind the wheel, belt up
and start the engine, though I am well aware
two hours down the road, we'll change drivers.

This is now the *modus* our road jaunts follow
because our bodies rebel against one position
for two hours. We stop, get out, walk around

for a few minutes, change positions, then drive
another pair of hours, until our bodies remind
us the time has come again to change drivers.

4.

Ah, but when I'm behind the wheel, the world
rolling by on the peripheral edges of my vision,
I am the closest to recognizing who I truly am:

I am my father for a time, viewing a farmer sowing,
surveying a herd of Angus grazing a clovered hill,
loving how a June wind ripples just-heading wheat.

I feel my father's smile form on my lips, as we
pass a pasture where a mare and two colts stand,
tails swishing mosquitoes, as they watch us pass.

I am my father, admiring the fresh coat of paint
glistening under August sun from a blue farmhouse,
neatly set on an expanse of fresh-mowed lawn.

My father and I are as one in our contentment.
If blood runs thicker than water, I drive with
and for my father—and we share this quiet joy.

My Father's Voice

My father had a great singing voice.
I have no memories of this of my own,
but one of my maternal aunts conveyed
this genealogical tidbit to me, and when I
seemed surprised, firmly insisted his voice
was not only beautiful, but that he knew
how to project it to good effect.

Yet somehow my father's voice appears
lost to me. I remember nothing of his
singing and when I learned about this,
my father had been dead a half-century.
Do I fail to remember his singing
because I never paid enough attention,
too absorbed in my own small world?
Or is it because my memories are
dominated by an older man who was
forty when he married, a man who grew
increasingly taciturn and introspective
as he neared the end of a life cut short
in his early sixties by bowel cancer.

I remember coming upon him at times,
hearing him humming to himself,
or often whistling in a tuneless fashion
only he seemed capable of appreciating.
But where is the beautiful baritone
my aunt adamantly insisted he had?
I have been a singer all my life, so I
assume I have my father to thank
for whatever musical talent he passed along,
though my thanks fall upon deaf ears.

This is just one of many regrets
about my father I have borne
since his premature leaving when I was
only twenty-two, regrets that time does
little to assuage, but makes more acute.
I have spent part of my life as a writer,
seeking and finding my own voice
and now, here, in my own latter years,
I sing less, write less, and spend time
pondering matters like my father's singing,
the inherent shortcomings of memory,
and a faint voice that lies somewhere
just beyond the rim of consciousness,
a voice I want so much to hear.

The Whistler

My father loved to whistle. When he was off alone,
working on one project or another, you might well

have been drawn to his odd, unidentifiable sounds,
before realizing my father was making them.

My aunt told me father had a powerful baritone,
but as he aged, he sang less and less, so I remember

little singing, much more of his whistling, which was
a different matter entirely. This whistling when he was

alone was by no means virtuosic. You might have
called my father a closet-whistler, unintentional,

the sound akin to praying or chanting, semi-tuneless,
at times reminiscent of the sound wind makes

when it set telephone wires thrumming. I don't know
when he began this private, toneless whistling, but I

do know he was capable, when he chose, to whistle
recognizable melodies, with a touch of musical verve.

I would happen upon him, and when he became
conscious of my presence, he'd stop his whistle-hum,

either speak to me, or busy himself with what he was
doing.
I never thought to ask about his peculiar whistling.

Some days my wife questions my humming sounds
and wonders why I can't just sing like normal people.

Gene-Gifts

Why do I keep writing these memories,
real or imagined, of my father, now gone
over six decades from my life?

Is there anyone left alive with reason
to doubt whether my own recollections
bear even slight resemblance to the man?

I can only tell you that though he left me,
a young man of twenty-two, about to embark
on a wondrous life with a wife and four children,

he always remained, unseen, but a presence
I could recognize in my own admonitions
or encouragement to my family, in my fears

and in my sadness. I have outlived his years
by two full decades, yet I know he is there,
though it seems he stands apart from me,

his blue eyes unflinching, as I recall them
in childhood memories. The year is not so
distant when both of us will become

simple memories of others, who may
or may not try to capture in words, what it
means to carry inside you the colour of eyes,

the manner of speaking, the tilt of the head—
all those traits one recognizes as having been
passed down to me, gene-gifts to the child.

Greening in the Year of the Plague

In a year that we have ear-marked
for quick dismissal from our memories
we manage to reach early May --
the greening of poplars and aspens.

No matter the fears and the fretting,
the disappointments and stresses,
that first faint tinge of chartreuse
is an elixir for the anguished soul.

As each day adds to the lemon-lime
unfolding, the beset heart surges with
reawakened belief that nature will
prevail, despite humans and viruses.

Shopping for Identity in Covid Times

Gone, it seems, are the days when
a Saturday morn at Safeway
could become a conversation with
a one-time colleague, or a former student,
resurrected from an earlier life;
or with a long-ago neighbour.

A pleasant Saturday morning
in a busy supermarket with carts
careening in every aisle, children
wheedling and whining, while
harried parents try to placate . . .
well, just no telling who might
pop right out of your past and be
standing just ahead of you
at the check-out counter, a smile
of recognition forming on their lips.

Such meaningful scenarios are rare
now, *verboten*. Faces hidden like failures,
shoppers mutate into masked hordes,
strangers scrabble over each other
in dumbfounding silence as they vie
for the product rumoured to be next
on the online hit list, Items to Stockpile.

I recognize no one in the store.
I get my groceries, pay and leave.
Who have I become?

Afternoon Chat

After two months of social distancing,
self-isolating, and living our lives as if
we were the last two humans left,

we visit with our long-time friends
who have also bungalowed themselves
in their own quarantine thoughts.

We meet in their backward for
BYOB glasses of wine, our two-metre
wines, as we call them; it seems

almost as if there is initial fumbling
for what we should say—a hesitance
to begin, *where do we start?*

as if perhaps we need to re-learn
the natural agenda-less chat:
what do we always talk about?

In the past two months of social
isolation, it seems our language
skills and usual glib small talk,

our quick, apt repartees have fled,
deserted us, become lost in a chasm
of discarded and forgotten words.

Stay in Touch

How often have we uttered
these words with friends or kin
as we bid them a safe trip,

then draw them to us, enclose
them a moment, as if we need
that physical certainty, the other's

heartbeat, on the unthinkable
possibility that this embrace
could be the last?

Perhaps it is our desire to keep
the ones we love safe by saying
stay, when we have already

acknowledged they must leave?
Stay in touch, we implore because
love is every bit as physical

as it is psychological or spiritual.
We should not need a pandemic
to verify the truth of this.

Blue Crabs, Galveston Bay

She slowly swings her woven circular net
into the Gulf that sloshes against rock slabs
of the elongated jetty on Bolivar Peninsula.

We stood, attentive to this tiny Asian crone,
while she knotted, as her ancestors taught,
a chunk of raw chicken into the mesh.

Further along the jetty, her two greying sons
cast lines into the bay, fiberglass surf rods,
afternoon sun flashing on expensive reels.

Now, crab trap at rest in the watery murk,
she sits back, content, on her rock to wait,
to sense movement below the rising tide.

We, too, wait and watch, curious, imagine
her great-grandfather whispering in her ear
minute details of foraging food from the sea.

The old woman rises, grasps the rope, draws
her net to the surface. *Aii-eee! A good one!*
She flips a large blue crab into the bucket.

What My Stylist Sees

This morning, while brushing my hair,
it occurred, as I parted the sparse strands,
that what I see in my mirror is not

the same perspective at all as that
of the woman who does her best
to restore order to what remains;

who attempts to convince me I still
have good reason to return each month
to accord my waning locks their due.

I sit in the salon chair while she stands
alongside, sometimes behind, as she snips.
She views my failing hair from a vantage

I cannot, each morning before the mirror;
no amount of artful brushing or combing
can disguise the fact that my hair is

in all-out retreat. She's seen this before,
of course—how men will do everything
within their power to delay the inevitable,

combing stringy clutches of sparse strands,
everything still extant on one side, upwards
and across plains of sunburned pate

to nestle gently on the other side like
a wispy coverlet casually tossed across
the bed. She's seen this subterfuge so often

she no longer needs to stifle a snicker,
but allows them their Samson delusions
and says nothing, just busies herself

with her buzzing clippers, feigning
a determined search for undetected strands,
or wispy tufts she may have missed.

Night Out

My friend and I lounge on bar stools
in a microbrew pub packed, wall to wall,
snug as brown bottles in cardboard cases
on a clattering bottling line. Din reigns.
Conversation loses to spittle exchanges.

We slowly nurse pints of hoppy lager
and survey the thronged table clusters.
Unwanted reality insinuates its way
to our stools—everyone here may well
be less than half our seventy plus years.
Some appear too young to vote,
let alone carouse. So, what are we doing
here—other than having a drink?
The bartender hovers: he wants to know
whether he should pour us another,
though we have several swallows left.

My friend dons his most disarming face
and murmurs, loud enough for the bartender,
We've been let out—a long pause—
for the evening, you know. . .
his eyebrows arch theatrically, wide-eyed,
as his voice slips into conspiratorial tones,
. . . and we're both off our meds tonight!

The young man guffaws, as if to say
he knows when his leg is being pulled.
Still, he edges away, glancing back as he
retreats to the refuge of safer patrons,
their heads bowed in discrete silence
over their androids and their I-phones.

Almost One Hundred

In the nursing care home Martha
cruises the seas in good spirits
towards her centennial birthday,

with staff members reminding her
regularly that she will reach
one hundred before too very long.

Occasionally, she will chirp loudly
to no one in particular, *I'm almost*
one hundred! Isn't that something?

A few of her fellow matrons smile
or nod in recognition of the feat,
though most remain mum, having

long lost track of their own ages,
unwilling or incapable of proffering
the slightest hint of their numbers.

So, Martha sails the seas towards
her centennial, tiny memories
jettisoned each day in her wake.

Morning Phone Calls

Most days, my friend calls me or I call him:
long-standing practice that may or may not
be unusual between two men. Whether it is
or isn't matters not a whit to either of us.

It's not as though we have unearthed
wondrous news; much of what we have to say
is banal, contrasted with riots, bombs, murders—
the daily human abuse filling the news.

We share the day's happenings and hopes
within that microcosm closest to us, the one
that means so much; a way of saying, without
utterance, that we are both hale and happy

enough to peel the rag-tag fragments
from our days, air them on the verbal lawn
in the light of day as close friends have
done for all time. It is not so much

the actual words, nor their multi-meanings.
It is voice and moment—small assurances
we need in an uncertain world, believing
there are still a few deep-rooted things,

a buffer against a murderous world that fills
us sometimes with despair; something we can
count on every morning, every day: a call,
a familiar voice, this sharing of our words.

Blood Test, 7:00 a.m.

Rising from the warmth of a duvet to face a blood test,
before morning's first coffee can pass your lips,

or the least morsel of food can boost your world,
before the show-off sun shakes up the eastern sky,

is not recommended for rational mortals. But here I am,
early morning, queued up outside the still-locked clinic,

with a motley of coffee-deprived grumps outside the
door,
waiting for the lock to unbolt, opening the dam to a
flood

of fasters, whose only non-violent thoughts are to get
inside, quick-bleed the demanded vials, then bolt back

home to an aromatic welcome of fresh-brewed coffee,
earthy toast, a favoured cup, waiting with the daily
paper.

Walker's Dilemma

Osteoarthritis has caught up to me.
I figured I could outwalk it, but failed.

I suspect the disease might have cheated
because I was known as a speedy walker,

a gait that sometimes surprised even me.
But it caught and passed me anyway.

Now, the next best friend to my wife
is my orthopedic surgeon, his syringe

of Depo-Medrol and Zylocaine to dull
the discomfort is the temporary relief

that keeps me buoyant. The surgeon is
patient, knowing eventually the needle

he provides will no longer fill the need;
new knees and hips are the future remedy.

Since I'm aiming for ambulatory nineties,
do I step up or slow down my pace?

Board Games

Rural youngsters, we grew up with a board game
called *crokinole*, though we never used that name.

We called it *caroms* because that's what happened
to our attempts to flick the circular game piece

where we were aiming. Our checker-sized wooden
disks would career off the upright pegs,

devilishly positioned on the board to thwart
all but the most eye-hand-coordinated among us.

It was frustrating then, as a pre-teen. And still is,
when our best attempts to be direct and open

with others, wick off pegs and sabotage our intent.
We carom haphazardly—through relationships,

through our lives—upset, but aware, as others
ricochet around us, we are not alone in the game.

Annual Medical

There I am, slumped on the edge of the examining
table,
book in hand, stripped to my boxer shorts, reading
poetry—
who knows how late my turn will arrive in the carousel

of medical appointments? Then my doctor raps once,
opens the door, walks in, shakes my hand and wants
to know, not how I'm feeling, but what I am reading.

A book of poems, written by a friend, I say. I pass it
to him,
he examines the cover, opens it, reads the inscription,
smiles,
then asks, *Which poem would you recommend I read?*

I find a poem, he reads, praises the vivid imagery. I read
a line from another poem about the sound of the strap
in the voice of a school principal; we agree it resonates.

When at last he addresses the reason I'm here in my
briefs,
he inquires how much walking I've been doing.
Every day,
thirty to forty minutes, I say. He approves. I tell him

Lincoln declared, *The best doctors you will ever see are*
your right leg and your left leg. He agrees, claims every
study
about the link between walking and health is
conclusive

about benefits. He says he enjoys biographies of
notables,
his favorite—Gandhi. Another—Lincoln; he
admires how
the famous president rose from poverty to greatness.

He says Lincoln's devotion to serving inspired him
to be
a family physician. I am thinking my annual medical is
shaping up as the first literary seminar our Medicare

will cover under the guise of an annual physical check-
up.
Just at that point, he slowly begins to stretch that evil
latex
glove up over his right hand. I roll over onto my side.

My Right Leg as Target

After the first few needles into my knee, numbers become irrelevant. Easy to lose count—six, a dozen? Just lie back and pretend it is entirely normal to lie supine on an examining table, here, in your vascular specialist's office, having some nameless saline fluid injected into your leg. Mundane procedure, ho-hum treatment aimed at reducing ungainly and unwanted expansion of the leg veins, a condition for which I can thank my mother's family genetics, though to be truthful, I haven't been all that thankful.

Today, the knee and upper thigh of my right leg is destined target area for this calm and cheerful, needle-wielding surgeon, who possesses lightning draw and meticulous aim, firing into the chosen vein locations, one round after another, quicker than Wyatt Earp at the OK Corral. Next, with brusque dexterity and brief dispatch, she attaches a small band-aid to each injection site, lassos my leg with a pair of large elastic tensor wraps. In a matter of seconds she is done, pleased, steps back, beams like a championship roper, over the trussed calf. "You're good to go. See you in six months."

Home for Sale

As we roll up the gravel driveway
that leads to your home,
            the first thing I see
is the vintage maroon Land Cruiser
parked in its usual spot,
            just off the driveway,
and the more upscale white Highlander
on the cement pad
            before the attached garage
inside which, last winter you
            established lavish quarters
for the several homeless cats that adopted you.

I stop our vehicle,
            shut off the engine and we
both just sit here, still,
a minute or two,
            as if we expect you
to open the front door
            and wave, your face
its usual beacon of joy.

            Of course, we know
that where you've gone
there is no waving
            at anyone or anything,

there is no one here to lead us
off on a stroll-around
to see the newest addition
to your own Sherwood Forest
gleaned from
online nurseries, local greenhouses,
box stores and supermarkets,
root-balled exotica
like the Weeping Norway Spruce,
to enhance your personal woodlot.

This May visit marks
eight months to the day
you left us
and though we know
you will not
burst from the house,
overflowing with exuberance,
with stories
you need to share,
today as we walk
one final time past your rose garden,
your summer pride,
soon to become the pleasure of someone else,
we know part of you
remains—and will,
whether we ever return—

in every root,
in every bloom,
in every thorn.

Retrievals

Some days memories refuse to come
up and out of that mysterious world
they rest in when you are no longer
paying them enough attention.

They stubbornly reject every form
of coaxing or prodding, content to lie
like clams, buried beneath distractions,
keeping a profile so low they vanish.

Even old photos won't do the trick;
on those days, photos of an earlier you
are of someone you might have met once,
perhaps at a long-ago party.

Photo of Boy and Dog, circa 1941

This snapshot is over eighty years old
and I am four, short pants held up with braces,

short-sleeved white shirt, a pudgy happy-faced goof,
one hand resting on the floppy-eared head of a mutt—

perhaps a Welsh Spaniel sire somewhere in the mix
of what my favourite uncle used to call *a dog party*.

This captured moment is from our Broadway yard,
a place I still walk in memory. I recognize the child

who still resides somewhere inside this aging body.
But the dog has disappeared. Without a wag or a bark.

A visitor's dog, no doubt, but why has it vanished?
That cheerful lad, soon to be off to a dog-less world

of school, where he would fetch pencils and books;
he would learn to stay, to sit and to stand on cue.

What the Photo Cannot Show

Two young brothers step towards the camera;
the older, perhaps five, the younger one,
not yet three. In their back yard their mother
clicks the shutter of the box camera. Eager
to protect his brother, the older reaches,
as if to steady that chubby wobbler.

The elder brother cannot know, but five years
after this photo, he will thrash an older, taller
bully for stealing his brother's cookie. Nor
can he know he will not be able to protect
him from the cancer that will snuff his life
four decades after their mother's snapshot.

Don't Talk to Strangers

I'm sitting in my car, motor idling, a back alley
in the downtown area, a winter day, temperature
minus 15 Celsius. My wife has dashed into
an art supply shop, unique for its back-alley entrance
and complete absence of parking, so I am illegally
    parked,
looking suspiciously like a getaway car outside a bank.
Waiting—suspicious or not. Good thing I have
all outward semblances of a harmless geezer.

A small child stands outside a nearby building
at a back door, trying to turn the door handle.
He has appeared there quite suddenly, an apparition—
no one was there, then this child: perhaps five or six,
a tee-shirt, bare head, he looks about ready to bawl.

I get out of the car, an icy wind grabs me, snow gusts.
I walk over, ask him if he needs help—
stating the obvious, I know. The boy shakes his head
and re-tries the door. His facial expression says,
"I can't talk to you. I don't know you."
I ask him how he got out here, where his parents are.
He's not eager to listen either. "Where's your Mom?"

Lucky, I've had three sons and eight grandsons.
I have seen this scenario many times in different forms,
though my telling this poor young boy won't make him
feel any better. He's done this to himself,
he knows it and it's written all over his face.
"She's inside the store," he blubbers.

I bang on the door loud enough to summon occupants
of an Egyptian crypt, let alone a rapt shopper.
"Does your Mom have a phone?
He nods again, his eyes becoming teary.

Another Samaritan arrives in the back alley
with a jacket to enwrap the little boy who is
beginning to shiver. "Do you know her number?"
He looks like he's about to lose it,
but he manages to spill it out and I call
the number, an out-of-province one,
on my cell phone. A woman answers.
"Are you missing a little boy?"

"*Oh, shit!*" is the only response. Moments later,
an adjoining back door opens, not even the same one
I have assaulted with my gloved fists,
the wayward child is snatched inside,
the door closes behind him.
The mother makes no appearance.

Life goes on. Snow drifts pass the moment
and then it, too, is gone.

Disappeared

One early farm morning
when I was about ten
I realized our farm dog
was not around.
Most unusual.

When I asked where
she was, I was told
she was not very well—
probably wandered away
during the night—
maybe coyotes
got her.

I knew she'd been
kicked in the head
by a draft horse
she'd determined
to nip in the heel.

What I didn't see
was a broken bone
above one eye
protruding
from her skull.

The dog disappeared
and never returned.

Within a week we had
a frisky collie pup,
cute and friendly.

I forgot the dog
that vanished—
until I became
old enough to know
farm dogs never
just disappear.

The End of Hostilities

When the Second World War ended,
I was eight, certainly aware enough
of the conflict to know which side
to cheer for, and that we were
on the side of good and right.
We lived in Vancouver and I
still remember the relief and joy
that enlivened the city when the end
of the war was finally announced
and our troops would return
to their families, though too many,
like my uncle, would not come back,
having been D-Day casualties.

I also knew the end of the war
would bring a welcome end to rations,
an end to the ongoing sugar shortage;
which in turn would mean we'd see
the reappearance of chocolate bars
and candies that had disappeared
from all our favourite confectionaries.

It also meant that mothers, shopping
the mostly sugarless supermarket shelves
for their families, would no longer
squabble and skirmish over rare jars
of strawberry jam or canned peaches.

No more rowdy grocery altercations,
no more split-and-bloodied scalps
from fracases over who had been
first in the queue for the rationed sweets.
The signing of the surrender in Europe
also marked a needed resumption
of relative peace on the home front.

Bulldozers

The bulldozers have come and gone.

Over days and weeks, they have
razed much of my childhood,
erased every trace—house, barn,
garage, every outbuilding.
Gone.

We inter our own history
under the sham mound of progress.

Every tree and shrub that burst
with songs of finch and thrush.
Animal paths that interlaced
the woods and held together each
small biotic world, connected
with its adjoining neighbours.
Gone.

Every fallen log, every hillock—
abandoned beaver dam,
or forgotten Indigenous grave—
levelled, each depression filled,
evened, to form a seamless bed
for some yet-to-be-determined
cash crop, to feed the future
with obliterated history.
Gone.

I hold onto these memories
the bulldozers could not find.
Each image will be buried with me.
Who then will remember—
now that the bulldozers have come
and gone?

Erasing History

Is this not where the farm of our youth stood?
Nothing here but canola field, right to the road.

Where are the fences, the gateway to the farm,
the garden, the rhubarb patch, the caragana hedges?

What happened to the barn Grandfather built of logs?
The sheds, the small wood frame house, the aspens

that sheltered us from bitter northwest winds?
Where have they gone? How can a ten-foot deep

farm dug-out disappear, as if it never existed,
as if it watered no cows, raised no ducks or geese?

A single farm, a thousand stories, grown fainter
and fainter until both stories and tellers are lost.

A blooming field of canola, a dazzle of yellow
beneath cyan sky, wind to tally gains or losses.

Hospital Waiting Room

Another man sits alone in one of the chairs
kitty-corner from me. He, too, has brought
his own book to mask the anxiety of the wait.

Somewhere removed, in a room we cannot see,
doctors and nurses exchange hospital gossip
as they perform their *scopies* on our wives.

On TV, Japanese forces count down the final
seconds before decimating America's navy
on December 7, 1941. Bombs will soon fall.

I am reading a collection of short stories—
an early Mayan potter's spirit interweaves
with a visiting woman from Saskatchewan.

A few chairs away a young Cree woman awaits
her *kokum's* return from wherever the nurse
has taken her, the twosome on first name basis.

On TV, the characters check watches or clocks.
In the waiting room time trudges. Locked
into our own fictional postures, we wait.

Bombs crash on Pearl Harbour, booms
of "Tora Tora Tora" fill the waiting room
and reverberate into the hospital corridor.

Kokum's grand-daughter, the other husband
and I read on, disconnected from Hollywood,
safe where no bombs will fall on us.

Elegy for Darrell Bell

The suddenness of it all was
so confounding—all those paintings
you never got to paint,
all the gallery shows
that will not happen—
only an incomplete painting world
remains, your finest landscapes
never envisioned, perhaps never begun,
just inner glimmerings of clouds on sky,
or light on water drowned
in sudden fall of darkness.

Here at our oak table, I admire how
your brush stroked this boreal lake
into being, into a perfection of motion,
colour and light, this painting
you created precisely for this wall—

"I know exactly what should go there!"—
knowing we loved the subtle mixture
of water, sky and light as much as you,
how pleased you were to be asked
to enliven and enrich our home
and our lives with the essence
of your life and art.

Wrenched too soon from us,
you leave unfillable emptiness.

Here, at this table, in this home we, too,
must share with time, I am lost
in your lake, in the memory of your smile,
your voice so close, that even if I am
thinking of Jan Lake right now, I know
you are there, too, your buoyant laugh
an echo of the exuberant joy
you brought to us all.

Naomi's Roses

Naomi's roses bloom through December.
They bloom from one year into the next,
through the assault on the national Capitol,
through the trial to impeach the President.

Naomi's roses bloom through snowstorms
that snuff blossoms, El Paso to Houston.
Austin shovels cars from under snowdrifts,
while snow flowers on Big Bend yuccas.

But in Naomi's garden, all is well—pink
and peach-toned roses wave and smile
at bees and migrating butterflies, smile
like spring sun lifting the wintery dark.

Excavation: Mount Pleasant Public School

This photo, circa 1940, struggles
to retain its original sepia tone,
now is more that of smog,
before the word had entered
the lexicon of Vancouverites.

This was my first school.
It is late fall or early winter.
Leaves have been raked, gathered.
Wind-stripped, pruned chestnut trees
guard the gate and the walkway
to where three brick storeys
loom in the greyness.

A woman on the sidewalk curb
looks across East Broadway.
Awaiting a streetcar? Two sets
of steel rails are visible
in the ample roadway, where
friends and I encouraged streetcars
to metamorphose in their passing
over-sized King George pennies
into strange thin medallions.

Is the woman waiting to cross
the street? To her left, a street lamp
is not yet on, though the day
is drab, between rains.
Or is it the antique photo's
dimming colour that conveys
a distinct sense of gloom?

The camera that chronicles
this moment has captured it from
the opposite side of the street,
from my home of seven years.

The bedrooms were second floor,
above street level. Was it
Mother's hand on the shutter
of a Kodak box camera?
Or was she the waiting woman?
Anxious for her son, who had
to cross the busy thoroughfare?

Behind this sole woman,
on the walkway to the school,
a cluster of several adults—
teachers leaving at day's end?

I cannot find myself here,
in this photo, nor can I see
other children. I imagine
places I might have been.

Mount Pleasant School is history,
long gone to wrecking ball
and the relentless bulldozers,
to the quick-tongued hucksters
of progress. What remains?
An old photo that will be
discarded someday soon,
if not by me, then by those
who survive me, who may reflect
for a moment, before relegating
the past to the shredder.

Lutheran Confirmation

Six people pose, south wall of a small prairie church,
which cannot be seen in its entirety—just one wall,

a single window, the assembled group. On the left,
far background, headstones, makers of church history.

Five teens in two rows, stand with the pastor, who
has vainly tried to instil in them Lutheran dogma.

Three boys, two girls—girls in front, hands crossed,
hold catechisms they have spent the summer studying.

Two boys, behind, only partly visible. The one on the
left,
seen entirely and he, too, holds a catechism in one
hand.

The hands of the other two are unseen. The youngest
appears to detach himself from the photo, tucked
behind

the two girls, both taller; his head is all that we see,
his face a mask, halfway between grimace and grin.

The confirmands look to the camera and
photographer—
not unhappily, but with implicit understanding:

they will soon finish this interlude and be called
 towards
matters more amenable to their desires, catechisms
 ditched,

consigned, with rote lists of Biblical names, to a musty
 niche
of memory. Of the six, the pastor seems least
 comfortable,

most difficult to read. His face radiates no pleasure
 or joy.
Perhaps the glare of summer sun as he looks at the
 camera

makes him want to squint; his mien, one of deter-
 mination,
or is it resignation? Perhaps he has recognized, inside,

where matters count most, that the five will soon
 be gone
from the watchful security of his flock into a dark world

in which his or any attempts at charting a safe passage
will end up being a waste of carefully scripted words.

Three Graves

My uncle insisted three Indigenous graves
were located on one of his grain fields.
He said they had become difficult to see
after decades of the cycle of cropping,
followed by summer-fallowing, before
again seeding the most current crop.

As a teen, I cultivated that very field—
sixty-plus acres lying west of the creek
that split the quarter-section into near-halves.
Perched on the tractor seat, I scanned
the field ahead for boulders or obstacles,
or the unexpected appearance of animals.

But I admit I was also determined to locate
the disappeared mounds that marked
the final resting place of three people
we never knew, who died long before
my uncle sowed his first wheat kernels
on land those earlier people knew differently.

Several times I'd stop, dismount, walk
to a spot that appeared, from the tractor,
to possess the imagined contours. Each time,
I climbed back up, and reseated myself,
disappointed. Still, I continued the quest.
In the right light, I was sure, I'd see them.

That was over seventy years ago. Those
graves remain there, where they've been,
unmarked and otherwise unremembered,
unless other family lore sustains them.
My uncle is dead, but those graves live
in my memory. I keep them for us all.

Before the Haka

Each time I see the Haka dance
performed by Kiwi soccer players
as a prelude to an All-Blacks' soccer match
on TV, I am whisked back
in time to my farm childhood.

We had a male, mostly border collie,
a generally friendly mutt,
an excellent companion for a boy,
but barely a middling help
with cattle, despite its breeding.
Herding cattle appeared absent
in Carlo's job description.

Carlo's most memorable trait turned out
to be its intense hatred of one neighbor—
and one neighbor only. This dog knew
always long before we did, whenever
that man would make an appearance.
The strange sound began deep
in the back of the animal's throat,
almost a low moan, growing in intensity
to a growl, moving from warning to rage,
as the aroused animal strutted,
stiff-legged as a cenotaph sentry,
back and forth around the yard
in an exaggerated display of canine ferocity.

By the time our ears had tuned in enough
to recognize the neighbour's tractor,
or in winter, his team of horses, the dog
had stoked its fury to the sticking point.
The collie, quite oblivious to Maori culture,
was mounting its own distinctive show
of willingness to defend its own turf
against unwanted or unfriendly intruders.

Language Borders

Sometimes, there are no words.
Nada. Rien. Zilch.

Nothing may come to the tongue
when circumstances demand
an acceptable, if not proper response.

But what is that right response
and do we always recognize it?

Perhaps there are good reasons
for when words do not come,
when the tongue becomes
a mute lump of coal.

Better no words at all
than words that sing
false notes, or words
with edges that wound,
and cannot be unsaid.

Not every silence
need be filled.

The Mushroom Woman

We came upon her in tiny Heritage Park, motionless,
peering down at a large mushroom that had emerged
overnight, inspired by yesterday's rainfall.

We had noticed and spoken with her previously,
enough to realize her knowledge of fungi, including
the outright poisonous ones, greatly outstripped ours.

She always carried her camera and focused on
capturing each particular feature of a fungus
to satisfy whatever her field studies required.

She was photographing a large, orange-hued fungus,
a showy specimen. "You don't want to eat this one!"
she offered, though we assured her the mushroom

she was engrossed in was one we already knew
was to be avoided. "*Amanita muscaria*," she added.
We nodded in agreement, though we needn't have.

The *amanita* name we recalled from past foraging,
both in the parklands and in our own field guides.
The amanita's beaming mask belies its deadliness.

We left her chatting amiably with another walker
and before we left the woods, we spotted several
more dangerous amanitas, their seductive facade

beckoning passersby closer, ever closer, to marvel
over their sudden allure, like storm-beset sailors
drawn to the allure of the Sirens of ancient myth.

Willie's Guitar

In the photo, Willie performs on stage
to mark his 80th birthday. Your eye is
drawn not to Willie, but to the decrepit guitar.
How can one of America's musical icons
appear with a guitar looking as though it
was rescued from the town dump?
Only the spectacular disrepute
of the ravaged Martin he plays
can distract us from how old Willie is.
How apt that this instrument he bought
in 1969 has stood both the test of time
and of the man himself, not without
considerable wear to both.
His fingers have beaten a hole
clean through the guitar face;
the hole widens with each playing,
then gets reinforced, buttressed,
and readied for another concert—
just like Willie. Each day he rises
with another song in his head, he knows
he's good to play his guitar another time.
Willie and Trigger as one, keeping
that final song at bay, one strum at a time.

The Street Cleaners

In the morning streets of Centro Merida,
the sweepers are already at work,
palm frond brooms in hand—
swish-swish, swish-swish—the sound
of human labour throughout the centuries.

Off the sidewalks fly cigarette butts,
gum wrappers, clear wrappings from
bakery sweets, furtive crumpled balls
of paper tissue dropped by a young woman
whose date failed to show again,
a Styrofoam coffee cup discarded
by the tourist who couldn't distinguish
ORGANICA from its counterpart.

Swish-swish, swish-swish, sing the brooms;
off the walk flies the trash, gathered
into a small mound, to await the wheeled
bin and the worker with the spade.

Bend and scoop, bend and scoop,
push the refuse onward into morning.
Swish, swish—down the street,
swish-swish, bend and scoop,
the grating trash bin at their heels,
wheeling them onward into the heat
of the day and to its end, when,
brooms set aside, they rest
in the arms of family.

Mariupol: March 2022

. . . a found poem, New York Times

1.

Here: the bodies of the children
dumped into this narrow trench

dug into the still-frozen earth
to the drumbeat of shelling

See, this 18-month-toddler whose
shrapnel head wound was too much

this 16-year-old, legs blown up
during a school soccer game

this girl, no more than 6, her pajamas
cartooned with unicorns, one of the first

of the children of Mariupol
to die from a Russian shell

2.

Their bodies stacked with others --
this mass grave on Mariupol's outskirts

Workers toss the bodies, tarp-covered,
or bedsheet-wrapped, weighted with stones

pile them as fast as they can: the less time
the better their survival chances

"Damn them all—those people
who started this!"
the worker rages as he
tosses a black body bag
More bodies will come:
they are everywhere—
corpses laid out, adults and children—
awaiting pick-up

3.

Mariupol, southern seaport of 430,000
now encircled by Russian soldiers

Food is running out, Russians have
stopped attempts at humanitarian aid

Electricity is almost gone, water sparse
residents melt snow to drink

Death is everywhere. Bodies can not
be counted because of constant shelling

4.

At the hospital an ambulance arrives
with a six-year-old girl and her parents

victims of Russian civilian shelling
Doctors huddle around her, but too late

"Show this to Putin!" one doctor fumes,
"The eyes of this child, crying doctors."

Part Two

Sunbeams and Shadows

Snowy Owl Snarls Traffic in Saskatoon

Where did you come from, splendid winged one?
Just passing through, enroute to fields teeming
with mice and voles, nocturnal vittles?

What a strange perch to alight, this asphalt patch
of road, the mayhem of motorists, here
in the driveway entrance to a shopping mall.

Look around, snowy star! You've managed
what even traffic lights rarely can with certainty—
backed traffic to a standstill with your presence.

A rare sight on any road at any time,
your sudden presence has changed the tenor
of the day, slowed the rush, brought the police

to direct traffic and ensure your safety, summoned
wildlife officials to attend your needs. This small
respite from the usual urban ennui, a news item,

a driver's anecdote, a curiosity, quickly forgotten.
Perhaps there's a smidgeon of comfort we can
glean from your unexpected visit: despite our failures,

our lack of will so often to do what's right,
this day suggests that hope manifests itself
in unexpected places, in wee but wondrous ways.

Crow Meditation

I.

After an absence of over five months,
the Crows are back, the flying bullies
have returned. They always do.

An April morning, you glance out your
window, expecting the same snowy
boredom you've witnessed daily.

But today there is a difference,
an unexpected one—Crow has flown
from the other side of the busy avenue,

lands on a lamp post and caws. Its beak
opens and closes, but inside your condo
you are left to imagine its harsh voice.

Your first Crow this spring and though
you would argue that Crows can be both
fascinating and entertaining, most people

do not rate them as elite subjects
among birds-to-watch. Crows tend
to languish in avian popularity polls.

Why then does spotting the year's first
of the coal-feathered outcasts bring a surge,
if not of joy, then at least satisfaction?

Is it confirmation of an expectation?
Or the assurance, here and now, Nature
has proclaimed again that all is well?

2.

Crow flaps off and away from its perch
and begins its methodical neighbourhood
patrol. How often have you been drawn

to observe their morning ritual, flying
from one perch to another as they undertake
inspection of territory they deem theirs?

You know that Crows are as aware of you,
standing at your window, as you are of them,
whether they are perched on the iron fence,

handy to their domain and to our condo's
communal property, or clutching a branch
of the Scots pine growing on the nearby berm.

You know, too, that Crows have an uncanny
memory for human faces and recognize quickly
which homes to avoid, which have harmless

bird watchers, which harbour stone-hurlers.
You wonder what Crows associate with you
when they recognize you at the window.

They watch you watching them. They have
deemed you tolerable, but remain ever wary,
accepting of your window presence, so long

as you do not interfere in any way with
the daily Crow business; and so long
as you stay on your side of the pane.

3.

Each spring, one Crow will always stop
at our back deck, perch on the deck rail
and stare pointedly at the empty spot where

Sonia had, several years before, installed
a burbling water fountain that gurgled
water for as many hours as she chose.

Crows remember. Each year they check
to discern whether she has altered her view
and forgiven them whatever indiscretions

they must have committed. The Crows will
be checking every year, even after we have
left this place, and strangers will have

replaced us. One day, a new face will
stand at this window, curious, bemused,
as omniscient Crow makes its daily call,

a face Crow will also come to recognize,
while the new face looks on curiously,
wondering when spring will arrive.

False Spring: February

The back of a two-week deep freeze siege
has been broken. From heated homes,

people emerge, tentative as Spring gophers
blinking at the sun. But it is not Spring

at all, the temperature still below freezing—
winter prevails. This brief respite from chill

stirs us all. A blue smear above and a skitterish
sun that skulks just above the southern horizon,

buoys us with a day parole from the cold
walls of winter. This warmth is ephemeral,

but listen—snow melt burbles its song
in the eaves, and we offer our tiny prayers . . .

Mid-Winter Waxwings

It is sudden—they appear, that's all.

You have not seen a single waxwing
since winter cracked its cold work;
then one morning your mountain ash,
loaded with bright orange-red berries,
metamorphoses into bustling birdfest
in the sub-zero weather, bursting
with the peaked cinnamon caps
of taupe-breasted Bohemian waxwings
with their bright yellow tail bands,
feasting on shriveled and shrunken
reddish berries they have ignored until
this bitter January day to harvest.

Why have they waited this long
to launch this feast? What have they
learned about the alluring ash berries
that they would forego the reaping
to this frigid day? What has nature
taught them, or how adapted them,
that these sociable banquet-goers
appear to be the sole creatures
to feast on the vermilion fruit?

This deep cold cameo appearance
when the rest of nature appears
both still and dormant is something
oddly rewarding; an electric surge
of excitement, even as you know
what you've witnessed is just a flock
of fifty common winter birds doing
what they must to survive prairie winter.
After they have stripped the last berry
from the tree and departed *en masse*
for tree sanctuaries elsewhere, you are left
alone with your growing sense of loss.

Norwegian Forest Cats

My friend owned a striking pair of forest cats;
or rather, two of them owned my friend.

Strutting fur-balls, they were so affectionate,
so socially interactive, the twosome seemed

to deem themselves dogs, but more intelligent.
And dog his steps they did, wherever he went,

eager for attention, flopping down, rolling over
on their backs, awaiting petting as their just due.

He called them his garden aides because they
unfailingly impeded any attempts to weed,

water, or tend to the nurture of his garden,
considering their own nurture a greater priority.

As outdoorsy as their master, the forest cats
came and went from the house as they chose,

their day, one of climbing trees and foraging,
those days they and he were not gardening.

My wife and I'd go out in May for rhubarb
in the garden of the forest cats and they would

cheerfully lead the way and entertain us, while
we cut and stacked spring-fresh rhubarb stalks.

Our friend's cats were so amiable I was tempted,
at least briefly, to find one for our own home,

at least until I was reminded cat fur ranked
near the top of my list of allergens to avoid.

Still, a garden with a Norwegian forest cat or two
is compelling enough I could convince myself

an occasional sneezing or coughing bout a small
price to pay for such elite companionship.

Red-winged Blackbirds

It's the twenty-seventh of April in the first
year of pandemic and we are hoofing along

the damp-from-yesterday's-rain path through
our local park and my legs are whimpering

independently, while my peevish back whinges
from some unspecified injury I've forgotten

when we notice several dark avian profiles,
perched on separate, socially-distanced aspens.

We hear the spring *kon-ka-reeeee* trill that
tells us red-winged blackbirds have returned

and are selecting vantage points from which
to tell us they are ready to reclaim dominion

over park ponds and reeds, red willow thickets
and the aspens, every perch and vantage point

from which epauletted males will shout macho
taunts about territory, nesting and the short

intense summer that begins the day they arrive.
There is no avoiding the brazen birds,

should you be so inclined. They are political
poets of the bird world and like Milton Acorn

they shout love, whether you understand,
or appreciate, or agree with it or not.

When March Unwinters Us

Early March morning and you arouse
to a shivering thermometer, an alert
that outside your insulated walls
the world, tugged from darkness
by dawn light, is silent and still
at -34 Celsius and you are prepared
to whine your oft-repeated,
but by-now familiar theme:
will this winter never end?

Though your rational mind may
recognize the sun is so much higher,
warmer now, so strong that snow
begins to melt long before the temperature
climbs above freezing, still the intense
longing for Spring seethes within.

Two days later the mercury creeps
above zero and the snow begins
its wondrous mystery of unmaking itself
before your eyes, sighing into itself
like cheeks on a denture-less man.
The hundred variant songs of water
are sounding in eaves and gutters,
evocations that vibrate the urgent air,
setting messages astir in wakeful aspens.

Hard to Love a Crow

The day my wife installed the multi-pooled
water fountain outside on our back deck,
I expect we both shared the same vision:

robins and sparrows, warblers and finches,
chickadees and other songsters would arrive
at our burbling flow to drink and to splash.

What joy we'd share, inside, only mere feet
away, experiencing effortless, comfortable
bird-watching, with no need of binoculars.

But over Eden, there hovered dark shadows
we hadn't anticipated. Crows were the first
to discover our cascading waterfall and bath.

Their wiliness often amused us as they dunked
dried bread crusts before carrying them off.
But we also recognized their black presence

cowed smaller species, so much so, our fountain
became the feathered bullies' private oasis,
which they commandeered with corvid zeal.

On the morning we watched one black assassin
dunk its breakfast, a robin fledgling, into the pool,
the chortling water was silenced for the summer.

First Leaves in April

There—Spring's first leaves --
newly-minted medals of green,

pinned and proud, on gooseberry canes
in Heritage Park this morning.

A gorgeous clear day, warm
enough at eight a.m. to make you

believe summer a mere heart-beat away.
I stand enthralled, as if somehow

this was all quite impossible;
as if the earliness of the season

had shifted the calendar awry;
as if the workings of Nature were

so mysterious, this verdant glitter
of gooseberry green against

the drab grey of winter dormancy,
with each leaf waiting its own turn,

one after another, to stun passersby
into an explosion of exclamations,

must surely be a mistake.

El Tecolote

We fell, almost instantly, into feathery dreams.

A late evening arrival in Merida, too exhausted
to even notice, until morning, our hotel had
christened each of their rooms with a Spanish name—
the sign alongside our door announced our room
was named for a small Mexican owl.

Perfect. I seldom go very long without
writing a poem through which birds flutter,
fly or soar, perch on roofs, or hoot
insistently from their leafy boughs.

El Tecolote has served us well: location perfect—
nearby courtyard greenery, open sky, no steep
climb to an imperial eagle's upper aerie --
but instead, a main floor room. Ideal.

Why is it when an owl flies into your poem
it wants to take over, despite your intent?
Owls are like that. Different-sized-and-shaped,
owls have always floated or swooped into my lines
when I least expect them. So why would I
doubt this would not hold true for *El Tecolote*?

Each time I stroll past our door sign, I love to roll
the five sonorous syllables around in my mouth,
while I imagine pointed ears, penetrating eyes,
large as those of a Great Grey, or Snowy Owl,
but this Hispanic version is an unimpressive brown.
El Tecolote, I still whisper in reverence.

In the courtyard I let my eyes flicker skyward
to scan roof-tops, urging the elusive owl
to transform from mellifluous syllables of Spanish
to the breathing certainty of feather and bone.

Merida, Yucatan, Mexico

Spring Juncos

The Ides of April and we are bundled
in warmest fleeces; windbreaker hoods
cowl our faces to thwart the nastiness
from a fierce northeaster shoving
this morning in the direction of ugly.

We round a curve and ahead, alongside
the path, winter's leftover grass is alive
and moving with hundreds of sprightly
grey clumps that become birds as we
draw nearer, then slowly morph
into a migration of jaunty juncos.

The morbid wintry thoughts we
have borne like weighty backpacks
suddenly dissipate in the perky exuberance
of several hundred slatey seed-eaters
breakfasting on autumn's leftovers.
The thought warms us: the juncos
have returned to us.

Late September Morning

You always hear them
before you see them.

When I heard them,
I stopped, looked up:

the cries of Snow Geese,
thousands of them,

ragged flying necklaces
strewn across

a robin's egg sky,
slant of rising sun

glinting off
brilliant white feathers.

That familiar ache
seized my throat,

their plaintive cries
waning as they flowed by,

carrying summer
southwest to the river.

Cooper's Hawks

"Cooper's Hawk, for sure," the photographer said,
when I asked him about the hawk he was
photographing,
the morning we chanced upon him in tiny Heritage
Park.
I doubt I can distinguish a Cooper's Hawk from
a Sharp-shinned one, or any other. He sounded
confident.

My wife and I had been watching this same hawk
family
for several weeks and we were far from alone in
curiosity.
These accipiters had become all-star inhabitants
of this grove—their chosen nesting site, now
a popular viewing site for early morning strollers.

Sibley Field Guide to Birds describes them as
"uncommon" and "solitary," but this adult pair had
chosen
an unlikely spot to raise their three or four hatchlings.
I remembered this sparse grove of aspens and poplars
was also the nesting choice for a pair of Long-
eared Owls
a few summers previous to raise three owlets,
who became notable photo attractions. None returned.

This pair of Cooper's Hawks have succeeded—
at least to this point—and if they survive the perils
of migration and do return next May, will the adults
come back to this same grove, or will they seek out
more secluded woods, well removed from
public parks and heavily tramped walking trails?

Could one of the current fledglings become the next
hawk to nest here? One of the many things we will be
following like a serial drama on our daily morning
walks.

Bones and Wings

... remembering Dr. Stuart Houston

One of the world's foremost experts on turkey vultures
dislodged a salmon bone from the back of my throat.

A dubious juxtaposition of such disparate facts,
I know, but stay with me here. The bone-remover is

an enthusiastic ornithologist and I can say this because
turkey vultures are singularly unattractive creatures,

of minimal interest to most normal people. I would
gladly catch the salmon I eat, if only I could do so;

while this man captures turkey vultures, harrowing for
anyone, not least a family doctor. This bird man

is a medical doctor of much renown, from a family
of physicians spanning three generations. I was

a young man when I ate the salmon steak; the physician
had just begun his distinguished career. While he was

removing the fish bone, I had no thought of birds, nor I
assume did he at the time. He may well have wondered

how someone could eat fish and not be aware he was
swallowing a bone. Nor could either of us know,

while he was extracting the bone, that birds
    would draw
us together again, gather us both beneath their wings.

The Days of a Mean October

October has been a cruel month
and this seems needlessly unfair.

If we can survive these days
of gathering dark, we could
set a record for coldest October,

a month to dismiss, in a year most
will jettison outright as well.

October brought winter winds
and minus Celsius that hinted
a switch of calendar pages

with November or December.
Crows, discouraged, left town.

Migrating songbirds, enroute
from boreal forests stopped only
long enough for a quick bite—

whatever they could scrounge—
and had disappeared by morning.

All the while, we have watched
wild animals, too, brace for cold,
with the wintry sun gliding low

to the southwest, bound for warmer
climes and unrestricted at the border.

Awaiting the Winter Solstice

We are sledding our treacherous way
to the nadir of daylight again.
Outdoors we tread with edgy caution,

even as the faintest semblance of ice
slows our steps, shortens them
as if walking a fine but treacherous line.

Those who can afford them have installed
their extra-tread winter tires
stacking summer's tires atop one another,

in a garage corner to grumble of usurpation,
and await the return of dry streets.
This is Saskatoon's obeisance to winter—

this rite of passing the tire wrench like a baton,
as winter jostles autumn to the sideline:
this reluctant but resigned exchange.

In beautiful Saskatoon, we cope as we must
with this sunlight shortfall, though
nyctophiles among us await the longest night.

118 Tundra Swans

I spotted him on my morning walk—at a distance, poised with binoculars, as he studied the waterfowl on the pond. We met and paused to exchange sightings. "Nice to have the birds back." I was saying the obvious—for him, but also for myself. The birdman mentioned driving out of the city to look for birds, stopping beside a small lake teeming with gleaming Tundra Swans. By the time he finished counting, he'd reached 118 swans. His tone was reverential. I could see him, binoculars trained on them, articulating numbers like a bingo hall caller. I kept thinking how tough a task—counting Tundra Swans without missing a few altogether, since birds, even on water, are seldom stationary, or doubling up and counting the same swan several times. But he reported precisely 118 swans and why should I doubt the number? I also considered whether he may have been more fascinated with the numbers themselves. Does the number 118 have any special significance? Perhaps he had an orderly mind, one for which the details are more important than the image he would carry away. Does numerical imagery enhance memory? What does it matter? Let him go on counting swans for years to come. And may I, too, be granted more chance meetings with someone willing to stand beside a prairie marsh awhile for no other reason than to count Tundra Swans.

Feathered Cosa Nostra

It's May and Canada Geese
have taken over and control
the entirety of Lakewood Park.

It's not so much that
the spring hatch has caused
their numbers to burgeon,

nor the new legion
of gawky goslings, which adults
are doing their goosely best

to tend and marshal
into some outward semblance
of avian respectability;

it's that these geese know,
with a certainty that verges
on outright obnoxiousness,

that it is they for whom
this park was created; it is they,
who have undisputed privilege

and unchallenged right-of-way
on every pathway, every golfing green,
on both emerald softball diamonds

and yes, even the soccer pitch.
It is all theirs—pity the poor fool
who seeks to dispute this fact

and thus incurs both the instant wrath
and the utter fearlessness
of the single-minded ganders,

who, as problem-solvers tend to be
both prompt and certain, though
utterly devoid of manners.

By November, the honkers have
disappeared entirely from the park
and the Magpie gangs think

they are in charge, but they know,
come April, the bossy flying Vees
will again resume command.

Mid-Winter

Cold: a remembered feeling
needs experiencing only once.
Forever after, reaffirmation.

Look out your window—
early light. Though you are
warm inside the comfort

of home, you still feel
the cold you know is there—
you know well why the man

trudging past your house
slews sideways a moment,
screws his face away

from the bludgeon of wind
that blurs his eyes, a blade
that cleaves to the bone.

December Afternoon

Three in the afternoon
early December dims
to a gloaming

desultory snowflakes
float and waft—
frozen confetti

outside our window
day's dullness
is ignited

by acrylic brilliance
as mega-flakes
of white

drift down against
gathering dusk like
fireflies alighting

on our pane-side
we listen hard
to silence

Corvid Hygiene

Crow perches on the top bowl
    of the water fountain
    on the back deck,
bends and drinks deeply,
    tossing its head back,
    to hasten the flow,
then bends to drink once more,
    head again thrown back
    to swallow deeply.

I watch through the window,
    perhaps six feet away,
as sun glints iridescence
    off glistening feathers.
As Crow drinks, oddly enough,
I see an ebony pumpjack
    bending and raising,
    bending and raising.

Crow now, its thirst slaked,
wipes its beak back and forth
    on the upper rim
    of the fountain bowl,
first, one side of its beak,
    then the other side,
    repeating until satisfied.
I don't know whether
    I should feel amused,
    or am I astonished?

Crow turns to the window,
    cocks its head at me
    and those dark eyes
seize mine for a moment.
    I'm positive Crow
    would like to say
something to me, something
    I'm not at all sure
    I want to hear.

Polar Vortexes

I suppose we can thank
meteorologists for this polar vortex
arrived overnight in Saskatoon—

after all, they coined the term.
But arrival is one thing; overstaying
like unwanted relatives is another

for which we will decline
further thanks here in mid-February,
not while we are subjected

to the indignity of hauling out
our bulkiest clothes—coats,
thermal socks, itchy wool scarves.

In the over-hyped cause of fitness
I should make a point of
bundling up for this vortex

and to sally forth to remind myself
of what winter on wind-scoured
open plains is truly like.

But I need no such reminder.
I have sworn a pact with myself
to do all within my powers

to avoid reminders. My oft-frozen ears
remember, as does the tip of my nose
and each frost-bitten toe,

O yes, they remember the teary agony
of thawing in the kitchen warmth—
each digit's painful protest.

Over the years I have frozen as much,
though not nearly for as long, as any
glaciated Danish mummies,

more than any frozen-toed,
super-tough outdoor rink stars
from Irkutsk in wind-raked Siberia.

Who wants to be reminded?
Let this Arctic iciness do its utmost.
Whatever its successes, it will

fail to either impress or entice me
to abandon the comfort and warmth
of where I am now,

just so that I may hear my boots
noisily scrunch the packed snow trail
through an aspen stand,

or along a snow-cleared sidewalk?
Where I'm heading, there will be
no polar vortex in the forecast.

Intruder

The red fox lolled on the manicured green
of our condo's back lawn like any domestic dog—

warm autumn afternoon, newly mown grass
tickling its nose, a fox-nap imminent,

if only those scathing villains looming above
in the shaggy blue spruce would spare their vitriol.

A mealy-mouthed mob of crows, newly summoned,
hurled dark invective at the unwanted visitor.

The black gang deemed this *their* territory,
now under egregious trespass from the sleek sneak,

alerting all within hearing of their unmistakable
umbrage
with the bushy-tailed rogue.

As the clamor reached its acme, the fox rose,
languidly stretched its length, and strolled off

and away in apparent unconcern, from the dark
rancor, now lapsed into sudden, satisfied silence.

Last Day of January

What perverse pleasure is derived from the simple act
of slashing a dark, determined X through the final day.

Give yourself a pat on the back: you've made it
once more
through the longest, coldest month of the year and
already

you notice the days' lengthening, the sun's
strengthening.
Spring approaches, you muse airily, though part of you

is muttering, *Hold on, hold on, don't get carried away!*
Part of you remembers February can serve up for you

twenty-eight cracked-bone days, sometimes twenty-
nine.
Still, getting to February is a small winter victory.

So, rip January from your calendar, shred it, recycle
the remnants, revel a moment or two in this triumph.

Morning Catbirds

Midway through our morning walk,
we are braked to a halt, to stand
motionless and watch a grey catbird,

the first we'd seen in years, flit
from path to safety ahead—
a dense thicket along the path

crossing the causeway intersecting
the park pond. Five feet away,
we watch the male skitter along

a branch, flash its rufous tail patch
in bold courtship display and utter
its strange kitten-like call.

The catbird studies us, its instincts
gauging how much it ought to be
alarmed. A quick background flicker

signals the female presence. Were we
near the nest of a mating pair? Or was
this male just a spring rogue

enticing a new mate? We left the pair
to settle their affairs as birds must,
no less than human voyeurs.

One-sided Conversation

A Bohemian Waxwing perches on an arm
of the small green ash. I stop. Grey-brown
is usually uninviting, but early sun-slants
can enliven even the muted slate tones.

A jaunty Blue Jay arrives, picks a seat
on the same ash, a few feet from the other
and begins to prattle, as jays are prone to do,
with neither provocation nor invitation.

Whatever the jay may ask or demand,
the waxwing remains mum, while the jay
flits, branch to branch, seeking, interrogating,
but receiving no apparent shred of revelation.

Frustrated by its companion's reluctance
to disclose a single morsel of useful news,
the jay utters a few squawks and flaps off
in search of a more receptive audience.

Eighteen Lines About Snow

Just a single flake
drifts slowly, softly earthward:
prelude to snowstorm.

Summer rains are loud,
but snowflakes are mute actors,
who shape the silence.

Some snowfalls consist
of giant geometric shapes:
brr. . . cold artistry!

The deck rail is topped
with three deep inches of snow
and it's still falling.

Who would have believed
that so many snowflakes fell
from such a bright sky?

Snow is a canvas
where nature leaves its stories,
coming and going.

Night Travellers

She begins to slow the car as the highway
approaches the descent into the river valley.
"Usually deer along this stretch of road."

In the pale wash of headlights, as if invoked
from the darkness, two mule deer in slow motion
step up the embankment, intent on crossing.

We follow our own lights, our own pathways;
deer and other animals follow theirs. If we are
fortunate, our ways do not conflict with theirs.

She shows the patience of one who is at home
with night's animals, slows the vehicle to a crawl.
The deer stop, heads up, spot-lit silhouettes.

They wait for us to creep past. "I see them here—
often. . ." is all she says, as we slowly continue
across the river, up the slope to the other side.

She does not begrudge this sharing her time,
this space and this night, with all of these
nocturnal creatures who must travel through it.

Aspens and Robins

Nearing Heritage Park, a little oasis
sandwiched between condo communities
I am aware of a hubbub—
a din of bird communions.

I realize the vocals pour *en masse*
from a lively chorale of robins;
I recognize the birds as they flit
limb to limb, branch to branch.

Midway through this aspen grove,
their foliage now mostly snatched
by October winds, I stop, take time
to engage with this unusual moment.

I've seen robins in migration before,
small flocks of fifty or a hundred,
stopping to rest or feed. But the scope
of this encounter—this feathered choir,

how many thousands, I wondered.
A joyous moment, witnessed perhaps
once a lifetime only, as a miracle --
this vocal tabernacle, everyday woods.

Chickadee Morning

The sky, this second last day of November,
is reminiscent of August blue, light wind
ruffling and rippling pliant needles
of the hardy young Scotch pine
that steadfastly overlooks our window,
as if it finds more of interest here
than we can muster most days.

Here on my side of the pane, I am
drawn to the furious fluttering
of a handful of chickadees, hopping and hitching
along the length of needled limbs and twigs
as if in determined quest. I imagine them
probing out frozen insects,
or eggs deposited several months ago.

Black-capped chickadees, predominant
feathered foragers of winter's skeletal trees
this sun-warmed morning, as we tilt
towards the last month of twelve
in this annual journey to the longest night
and the official declaration
of winter, our six-month season.

The sun has fled the white plains
for more festive fields of play, abandoning
these hardy little birds, now busy
cleaning this conifer of insect detritus,
unopposed by bird bullies, watched only
by those who by choice or chance remain
here to muse and to mull over how
we have been abandoned
to our own winter thoughts.

Moonlight Foxes

The night is breathtakingly clear. We near home
after dining with friends and as we begin to round
the curve of Lakewood Park on Heritage Crescent,
I spot the shapes just below the snow embankment
to the left; they plan to cross the road to patrol
the pocket park on the other side of the crescent.

"Slow down! Foxes!" I call out to Sonia, who is
behind the wheel tonight. The foxes have
already made their decision and have retreated,
scrambled
back up the snowplowed mounds, gained the safety
of the sidewalk, where they stand, side by side,
alert, awaiting a less-pressed crossing of the road.

We roll slowly past the twosome. Intense moonlight
and the peripheral reaches of the headlights reveal,
even in the dimness of dark winter, the vividness
of their red-umber fur, their long luxuriant tails
as they stand, confident and easy, in the moonlight.

Two young foxes watch, patient but cautious,
as we pass, then resume their intended crossing,
unhurried as foxes tend to be, and continue
their patrol of territory their birth has granted
them in this urban neighbourhood of Saskatoon.

Red Fox Winter

The red fox treads slowly
in the new-fallen snow,
stops, listens, intent

Its perked ears detect
the scurry of small feet
below the snow crust

The predator visualizes
its prey, now motionless
on its well-trod route

A fox leap is pure ballet,
an arcing, head-first bolt
diving beneath the snow

and emerging in a white
shower of fine flakes,
a fresh meal in its jaws

Winter Sun

O wan sun of southern sky,
at two this January afternoon
you are more a memory
than dynamic distant star—

a paltry, faltering knock-off
of vigorous suns past, rather
than any vital source
of desired heat and comfort.

Weak though you appear,
we look to you with hope,
self-deluded that if we
avoid disparaging your

winter frailty, do and say
what is positive and proper,
and if we do not transgress
some universal law, the odds

must surely be on our side
for survival once again
through yet one more
brain-jangling January.

Acknowledgments

Most of the poems in this book appeared in earlier versions in the following print or online literary magazines or journals. The author wishes to thank all the editors and their readers for their yeoman service in bringing poetry and readers together. Many of the poems have appeared in *Amarillo Bay*, *Banyan Review*, *Bindweed Magazine*, *Blue Nib*, *Contemporary Review India*, *Devour: Art and Lit Canada*, *Dime Show Review*, *Foxglove Journal*, *Grain*, *Juniper Poetry*, *Keep Poems Alive*, *Moving Force Journal*, *Now Then Magazine*, *Manchester*, *Peacock Journal*, *Poetry Quarterly*, *Poetry Pause*, *Provo Canyon Review*, *Queen's Quarterly*, *River Volta Review*, *The Journal* (UK), *Triadae Magazine* (Spain), and *Your Daily Poem.*

"When March Unwinters Us" appeared on the website of the Parliamentary Poet Laureate of Canada, Michel Pleau, as "Poem of the Month," August, 2015.

In addition, several of the poems of this book have appeared in the following anthologies: "Afternoon Chat" in *Yellow Flag Poems*, San Antonio Arts Alive, as well as in *We Are One: Poems from the Pandemic*; "El Tecolote" and "The Street Cleaners" in *The Beauty of Being Elsewhere*, Hidden Brook Press, Brighton, ON; "Shopping for an Identity" in *True Identity*, Hidden Brook Press, Brighton, ON; "Snowy Owl Lands in Saskatoon" in *Poems to Lift You Up and Make You Smile*, Parson's Porch & Co, Cleveland; "Blue Crab, Galveston Bay" and "A Straightener of Nails" in *Tamaracks: Canadian Poetry for the 21st Century*, Lummox Press, San Pedro, California; and "Night Out" in *A Literary Harvest: Canadian Writing About Wine and Other Libations.*

The author also wishes to express his thankfulness and appreciation to his first reader, sharp-eyed editor, and enduring partner, Sonia. He is also indebted to the encouragement and ongoing editorial acumen of fellow writer and friend, Dave Margoshes. Without Edward Willett and his deep and determined belief in writing from Saskatchewan, this book may not have come to fruition.

About the Author

Glen Sorestad's poems have been appearing in print for more than fifty years. His poems have been presented in literary publications, in print and online, across North America and in many other countries, while being translated into at least eight languages. Among his many poetry books are two bilingual volumes, one English/Spanish and one English/Italian. Sorestad was named Saskatchewan's first Poet Laureate in 2000, becoming Canada's first provincially appointed Poet Laureate. He also spent twenty-five years as a co-founder and president of Thistledown Press, one of Canada's premier literary publishers. In 2010 he was appointed a Member of the Order of Canada. Sorestad and his wife Sonia live in Saskatoon. *First Light, Last Light* is his seventeenth book of poems.

About Shadowpaw Press

Shadowpaw Press is a traditional publishing company, located in Regina, Saskatchewan, Canada and founded in 2018 by Edward Willett, an award-winning author of science fiction, fantasy, and non-fiction for readers of all ages. A member of Literary Press Group (Canada) and the Association of Canadian Publishers, Shadowpaw Press publishes an eclectic selection of books by both new and established authors, including adult fiction, young adult fiction, children's books, non-fiction, and anthologies, plus new editions of notable, previously published books in any genre under the Shadowpaw Press Reprise imprint.

Email: publisher@shadowpawpress.com.

facebook.com/shadowpawpress
x.com/shadowpawpress
instagram.com/shadowpawpress

More from Shadowpaw Press
Available Now or Coming Soon

Literary Fiction

Hello by David Carpenter

Theories of Everything by Dwayne Brenna

The Laundryman by Dwayne Brenna

Elephants in the Room by Betty Jane Hegerat

Thickwood by Gayle M. Smith

Let us be True by Erna Buffie

The Lavender Child by Harriet Richards

Waiting for the Piano Tuner to Die by Harriet Richards

Dollybird by Anne Lazurko

Small Reckonings by Karin Melberg Schwier

Poetry

The Door at the End of Everything by Lynda Monahan

The Glass Lodge: 20th Anniversary Edition by John Brady McDonald

Phases by Belinda Betker

Stay by Katherine Lawrence

Literary Nonfiction

Tales This Side of the Elysian Fields by Trevor W. Harrison

Cupboard Love: A Dictionary of Culinary Curiosities by Mark Morton

The Crow Who Tampered With Time by Lloyd Ratzlaff

Backwater Mystic Blues by Lloyd Ratzlaff